THE ROMNEY, H
DYMCHURCH RA
by Jonathan James

Front Cover No.1 GREEN GODDESS departing from New Romney with a train to Hythe on 21 August 2015.
Jonathan James

Back Cover No.9 WINSTON CHURCHILL near Romney Sands on a busy summer afternoon on 20 August 2015.
Jonathan James

Above No.10 DR SYN resting between workings under the train shed at New Romney on 31 May 2014.
Jonathan James

Published by Mainline & Maritime Ltd
3 Broadleaze, Upper Seagry, near Chippenham, SN15 5EY
Tel: 07770 748615
www.mainlineandmaritime.co.uk   orders@mainlineandmaritime.co.uk
Printed in the UK
ISBN: 978-1-900340-84-7

Introduction

Although I grew up in south London, our family holidays were often taken at Camber Sands in East Sussex. Thanks to my grandfather, who was a railway enthusiast, our holidays often included a visit to the Kent and East Sussex Railway and the Hastings Miniature Railway. We also visited the Romney, Hythe and Dymchurch Railway, which was usually combined with a day on the beach at Dymchurch or a visit to the lighthouse at Dungeness.

I have returned to the railway many times over the years, with every visit being different. In more recent years I have taken my children for a ride on the railway and to the sandy beach and funfair at Dymchurch, which I loved so much as a child.

The Coronavirus pandemic has had a significant impact on the railway during 2020, although trains were able to operate during the summer with a special timetable in operation. Hopefully 2021 will see a return to more normal operations.

I would like to thank Peter Scott for providing the map included in this book.

There have been many books devoted to the Romney, Hythe and Dymchurch Railway over the years, but I hope you will enjoy my take on this fascinating railway.

Jonathan James

The Transport Trust have designated the Romney, Hythe and Dymchurch Railway a Transport Heritage Site.

The sign reads *'Opened 1927 as 'The smallest public railway in the world' and operated continuously, with original infrastructure and locomotives, ever since'.*

The sign is located outside of the café at New Romney and is seen here on 7 October 2018.

Jonathan James

Me and my sister Natalie admiring No.6 SAMSON at New Romney, probably around 1975.

My late grandfather Len Lambert standing alongside No.5 HERCULES in July 1971.

A Brief History Of The Railway

The Romney, Hythe and Dymchurch Railway was the brainchild of John Edwards Presgrave Howey (Captain Howey) and his friend, and fellow racing driver, Count Louis Zborowski. The two friends shared an interest in miniature railways and both constructed miniature railways in the grounds of their homes.

Sadly, Count Louis Zborowski was killed in a motor racing accident, so Captain Howey decided to proceed alone.

A number of sites were considered for a railway, before settling on the Romney Marsh. The dream was to build a 'Main Line in Miniature', and once that a Light Railway Order had been received, construction started between Hythe and New Romney. The railway was constructed to a gauge of 15 inches.

The first section of the railway opened on 16 July 1927, with the locomotives designed by Henry Greenly, who also managed the construction of the railway. A further Light Railway Order was obtained, which enabled the railway to be extended to Dungeness, which opened to The Pilot on 24 May 1928 and Dungeness on 3 August 1928. The whole route from Hythe to Dungeness was constructed with double track, except for a balloon loop at Dungeness.

The railway was taken over by the military during World War II and an armoured train, fitted with two machine guns and an anti-tank rifle, was created utilising No.5 HERCULES and two wagons. The railway also played a part in the PLUTO (Pipe Line Under the Ocean) project to supply fuel to support Operation Overlord, the Allied invasion of Normandy.

Following the war, the railway was found to be in a poor state of repair, resulting in the second track between New Romney and Dungeness being removed. In 1974 a passing loop was provided at Romney Sands to enable a more intensive service to operate on this section of the railway.

The railway ran into financial issues in the late 1960s / early 1970s and at one point it looked likely to close, but a consortium of railway enthusiasts took over the operation of the line. A number of other changes have taken place over the years, including the reconstruction of New Romney station in the early 1970s and the closure of some of the smaller Halts in 1977.

The railway today remains largely unchanged, with all of the original locomotives still in service, supplemented by some more modern additions. The stations themselves have been modernised over the years, partly to keep up with modern requirements, but the essence of the original 'Mainline in Miniature' still remains.

The Romney Marshes remain popular with visitors from the UK and abroad, with the market town of Hythe remaining a popular destination, contrasting with the beaches and fun fair at Dymchurch and the bleak nature reserve at Dungeness.

A mock-up of the armoured train at New Romney on 15 July 2015.

Jonathan James

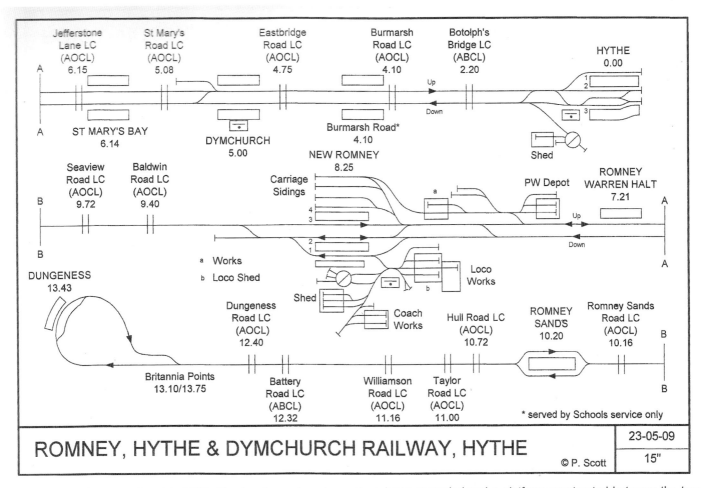

A map of the railway produced in 2009. The level crossings have since been upgraded and a platform constructed between the two tracks at Dungeness station.

Copyright Peter Scott

The view from a train approaching the 'tunnel' under the main road at New Romney on 19 August 2015. There are several overbridges along the line.

Jonathan James

A Trip Along The Line

Hythe is located on the edge of the Romney Marsh and was once one of the Cinque Ports, which were a confederation of ports along the Kent, Sussex and Essex coastlines. Hythe is also the starting point for many passengers visiting the Romney, Hythe and Dymchurch Railway. There is an impressive station building with an excellent gift shop and a café alongside. The station has an overall roof and three platforms, with a release road between platforms 2 and 3. There is also a turntable, signal box and a small shed.

No.12 J.B. SNELL preparing to depart from platform 3 at Hythe station on 14 April 2017. At one time there was a fourth platform to the right of the train. Freight traffic operated for a few years, conveying shingle from near Maddieson's Camp and fish traffic from Dungeness to Hythe, where there was a siding and unloading area.

Jonathan James

No.9 WINSTON CHURCHILL negotiating the reverse curves on the approach to Hythe on 14 April 2017.

Jonathan James

No.12 J.B. SNELL with a Dungeness bound train near Burmarsh Road on 14 April 2017.

Jonathan James

Burmarsh Road station is four miles from Hythe and is seen here on 21 August 2015. The station is no longer used on a regular basis after the regular school traffic ceased in July 2015. There were once two halts between Hythe and Burmarsh Road called Prince of Wales Halt, which closed in 1928, and Botolph's Bridge Halt, which closed in 1939.

Jonathan James

The railway has two tracks between Hythe and New Romney and is dead-straight on the approach to Dymchurch. Dymchurch station is five miles from Hythe and has a short siding at the New Romney end of the station. At one time the station had a third platform, which was intended for a shuttle service to New Romney, as well as a turntable and signal box. No.5 HERCULES is seen arriving at Dymchurch from Hythe on 7 May 2018, crossing Eastbridge Road level crossing and a small stream before reaching the platform.

Jonathan James

After leaving Dymchurch, the next station is St Mary's Bay, although there was once a private station in between, called Golden Sands Halt, although trains did not call on a regular basis, and after briefly being renamed Reunion Halt, it closed in the 1990s. No.10 DR.SYN approaching St. Mary's Bay from the New Romney direction on 14 April 2017.

Jonathan James

The next stop after St Mary's Bay is Romney Warren Halt, which only opens for special events and serves the Romney Marsh Visitors Centre. The halt reopened in 2009, close to the site of a previous halt. No.6 SAMSON arriving at Romney Warren Halt on 7 October 2018, whilst working a special train for the Narrow Gauge Railway Society.

Jonathan James

The next station is New Romney, just over eight miles from Hythe, which is also the railway headquarters. The locomotive and carriage sheds are also located at New Romney along with a café, shop, museum and model railway. The station is controlled from a small signal box. New Romney has four platforms covered by an overall roof. No. 9 WINSTON CHURCHILL approaching New Romney on 7 August 2015.

Jonathan James

No.10 DR SYN approaching New Romney from Dungeness on 14 April 2017.

Jonathan James

No.7 TYPHOON is seen here shortly after leaving New Romney on 17 August 2015, passing the site of the former main line station. There was once a platform here, sometimes known as Littlestone-on-Sea, which provided an interchange between the RH&DR and the national network. The track on the right is a siding, which is the remaining part of the double-track line that once existed between New Romney and Dungeness.

Jonathan James

Until 1983 there was a station called Greatstone (also known as Greatstone Dunes or Greatstone Halt). It was originally quite a large station, but the expected traffic did not materialise and it eventually closed. This is a view of an old army pillbox, which marks the former station site, seen on 14 April 2017.

Jonathan James

No.10 DR.SYN approaching Romney Sands, which is just over ten miles from Hythe, on 18 August 2015. The line here once had double-track, but it was damaged during World War II and never restored.

Jonathan James

No.14 CAPTAIN HOWEY approaching Romney Sands from Dungeness on 20 August 2015.

Jonathan James

No.7 TYPHOON crossing Seaview Road level crossing on 20 August 2015.

Jonathan James

No.9 WINSTON CHURCHILL crossing Hull Road level crossing on 30 May 2014.

Jonathan James

Between Romney Sands and Dungeness there are five level crossings. There were also two halts at Lade and The Pilot, both of which officially closed in 1977, although trains occasionally called for a few years afterwards. Dungeness station is located on a large balloon loop with the line dividing at Britannia Points. For a short period of time there was a halt at Britannia Points. No.4 THE BUG and No.6 SAMSON are seen approaching Britannia Points on 7 October 2018.

Jonathan James

No.14 CAPTAIN HOWEY approaching Dungeness on 21 August 2015. Dungeness is 13½ miles from Hythe. The station has a passing loop, shop and café. Dungeness also has a lighthouse, nature reserve and nuclear power station.

Jonathan James

The remains of a Fisherman's Railway at Dungeness, seen here on 21 August 2015. A number of these railways, of varying different gauges, operated at Dungeness and a number remain in various states of decay.

Jonathan James

Locomotives

The Romney, Hythe and Dymchurch railway has twelve passenger locomotives, including two diesel locomotives. Number 4, THE BUG, is also occasionally used on passenger services, either coupled to another locomotive or working a short train, including occasional shuttle services between New Romney and Romney Warren Halt. There are also three maintenance vehicles numbered PW1 to PW3.

No.	Name	Type	Builder	Built
1	GREEN GODDESS	4-6-2	Davey Paxman & Co	1925
2	NORTHERN CHIEF	4-6-2	Davey Paxman & Co	1925
3	SOUTHERN MAID	4-6-2	Davey Paxman & Co	1926
4	THE BUG	0-4-0T	Krauss	1926
5	HERCULES	4-8-2	Davey Paxman & Co	1927
6	SAMSON	4-8-2	Davey Paxman & Co	1927
7	TYPHOON	4-6-2	Davey Paxman & Co	1927
8	HURRICANE	4-6-2	Davey Paxman & Co	1927
9	WINSTON CHURCHILL	4-6-2	Yorkshire Engine Company	1931
10	DR.SYN	4-6-2	Yorkshire Engine Company	1931
11	BLACK PRINCE	4-6-2	Krupp	1937
12	J.B. SNELL (formerly JOHN SOUTHLAND)	Bo Bo	TMA Engineering	1983
14	CAPTAIN HOWEY	Bo Bo	TMA Engineering	1989
PW1		4wDM	Motor Rail Limited	1938
PW2	SCOOTER	0-4-0PM	RH&DR	1949
PW3	RED GAUNTLET	0-4-0PM	Jacot / Keef	1964 / 1975

No.1 GREEN GODDESS seen at New Romney on 17 August 2015.

Jonathan James

Two views of No.2 NORTHERN CHIEF at Romney Sands on 30 May 2014.

Jonathan James

No.3 SOUTHERN MAID arriving at New Romney on 14 April 2017.

Jonathan James

No.3 SOUTHERN MAID being prepared for service in the yard at New Romney on 7 October 2018.

Jonathan James

No.4 THE BUG being prepared for service at New Romney on 7 October 2018.

Jonathan James

No.4 THE BUG at New Romney on 14 May 2000.

Jonathan James

No.5 HERCULES on the turntable at Hythe on 10 March 2007.

Jonathan James

No.5 HERCULES preparing to depart from Dungeness on 7 May 2018.

Jonathan James

No.6 SAMSON arriving at Dymchurch on 15 July 2012.

Jonathan James

No.6 SAMSON and No.12 J.B. SNELL arriving at Dungeness on 7 October 2018.

Jonathan James

No.7 TYPHOON arriving at New Romney on 21 August 2015.

Jonathan James

No.7 TYPHOON preparing to depart from Dymchurch on 10 March 2007.

Jonathan James

No.8 HURRICANE shunting at New Romney on 14 April 2017.

Jonathan James

No.8 HURRICANE arriving at Dymchurch on 19 August 2015.

Jonathan James

No.9 WINSTON CHURCHILL on the turntable at Hythe on 14 April 2017.

Jonathan James

No.9 WINSTON CHURCHILL at New Romney on 10 May 2008.

Jonathan James

No.10 DR SYN standing at Dungeness on 14 May 2000.

Jonathan James

No.10 DR SYN at Romney Sands on 1 June 2014.

Jonathan James

No.11 BLACK PRINCE standing at New Romney on 14 May 2000.

Jonathan James

No.11 BLACK PRINCE at New Romney on 31 May 2014.

Jonathan James

No.12 JOHN SOUTHLAND at New Romney in August 1986.

Jonathan James

No.12 JOHN SOUTHLAND, later renamed J.B.SNELL, arriving at Dymchurch on 25 July 1999.

Jonathan James

No.14 CAPTAIN HOWEY in the yard at New Romney on 14 May 2000.

Jonathan James

No.14 CAPTAIN HOWEY at Hythe on 20 August 2015.

Jonathan James

PW1, built by Motor Rail Limited, shunting at New Romney on 17 April 2003.

Jonathan James

PW1 at New Romney on 7 October 2018.

Jonathan James

PW2 in War Department livery, outside the sheds at New Romney on 10 May 2008.

Jonathan James

PW2 inside the Permanent Way shed at New Romney on 7 October 2018.

Jonathan James

RED GAUNTLET outside the Permanent Way shed at New Romney on 10 May 2008.

Jonathan James

Visiting Locomotives

4-6-0 Black Five number 5305, built by Austin Moss, at New Romney on 14 May 2000.

Jonathan James

American Switcher No.712, built by R.H.Morse, at New Romney on 14 May 2000.

Jonathan James

SIAN, a 2-4-2 built by Guest Engineering in 1963 for the Fairbourne Railway, outside the loco sheds at New Romney on 14 May 2000.
Jonathan James

SHELAGH OF ESKDALE, a diesel locomotive built by Severn Lamb in 1969, visiting from the Ravenglass and Eskdale Railway, seen here at Dungeness in summer 1982.

Jonathan James

PHYLLIS is a guard's van and wheelchair coach built in 2015, seen here at Hythe on 14 April 2017.

Jonathan James

Coach number 807, built in 1969, seen here at Hythe on 14 April 2017.

Jonathan James

Coach Number 61, built in 1975, seen here on 14 April 2017.

Jonathan James

Clayton Pullman coach number 110, built in 1928, at New Romney on 10 May 2008.

Jonathan James

Coach number 105 MARJORIE is a wheelchair coach, seen here at New Romney on 7 October 2018.

Jonathan James

Another view of coach 105 MARJORIE at Hythe on 21 August 2015.

Jonathan James

Coach 805, built in 1971, at Hythe on 15 July 2012.

Jonathan James

Coach 455, built in 1986, in use by the permanent way department, in the sidings at New Romney on 14 April 2017.

Jonathan James

Permanent way wagons 100P and 205P at New Romney on 31 May 2014.

Jonathan James

An ex 4-wheel passenger carriage now used by the permanent way department at New Romney on 14 April 2017.

Jonathan James

Wagon number 263 'Ricky' in the permanent way shed on 7 October 2018.

Jonathan James

Some of the old tipper wagons in the sidings at New Romney on 31 May 2014.

Jonathan James

Hythe station building seen here on 14 April 2017.

Jonathan James

The signal gantry and signal box at Hythe, on the same date.

Jonathan James

The train shed at Hythe seen on 14 April 2017.

Jonathan James

No.14 CAPTAIN HOWEY shunting under the train shed at Hythe on 21 August 2015.

Jonathan James

The station building at Dymchurch, which occupies the site of the former bay platform, taken on 19 August 2015.

Jonathan James

A view of Dymchurch station looking towards New Romney taken on 14 April 2017. The station once had an overall roof, but this was removed in 1979.

Jonathan James

A view of the footbridge at Dymchurch, looking towards Hythe, with the station toilets located in the bridge piers, seen here on 14 April 2017.

Jonathan James

St Mary's Bay is generally unstaffed, with the ticket office only usually open for special events. The view here is looking towards Hythe, taken on 12 April 2017.

Jonathan James

No.10 DR. SYN arriving at St Mary's Bay on 14 April 2017.
Jonathan James

The 2017 timetable for St Mary's Bay, with a small 'r' indicating that trains stop by request only. Taken on 14 April 2017.
Jonathan James

The platform at Romney Warren Halt taken on 14 April 2017.

Jonathan James

No.2 NORTHERN CHIEF and No.14 CAPTAIN HOWEY, viewed from under the trainshed at New Romney on 31 May 2014.

Jonathan James

New Romney station building at road level, seen here on 30 May 2014.

Jonathan James

A view of the trainshed looking towards Hythe from the footbridge, taken on 21 August 2015.

Jonathan James

A view of New Romney station taken on 17 August 2015. The station has four platforms these days.

Jonathan James

No.1 GREEN GODDESS departing from Romney Sands towards Hythe on 20 August 2015, passing the ticket office and adjacent camp site.

Jonathan James

No.14 CAPTAIN HOWEY standing in the rain at Romney Sands on 18 August 2015.

Jonathan James

No.8 HURRICANE at Dungeness on 19 August 2015 before the additional platform was added.

Jonathan James

A view of the new station at Dungeness, including the additional concrete platform laid between the two tracks, taken on 7 October 2018.

Jonathan James

No.4 THE BUG seen at Dungeness with a Narrow Gauge Railway Society special on 7 October 2018, with the new station building and platform in view.

Jonathan James

Timetables

A winter service usually operates on most weekends in November and January, between New Romney and Dungeness, usually consisting of three return trips.

Santa Specials operate at weekends from late November and through to Christmas, with extra services on Christmas week.

Weekends during February and March usually consist of a full service between Hythe and Dungeness, supplemented by weekday services during school holidays.

From Easter to October services usually operate every day, with enhanced services when special events are taking place.

The high-peak timetable, which usually operates during the school summer holidays, consists of ten trains each way along the full length of the line, with a few short workings between Hythe and New Romney and Dungeness and New Romney at the start and end of the day.

Tickets

Electronic printed tickets are provided from the ticket offices. In 2020 the all-day adult rover ticket cost £19.00 (£9.50 for a child), with a family ticket costing £52.00.

Shops and Cafes

There are gift shops at Hythe, New Romney and Dungeness. Dymchurch and Romney Sands stations also hold a small stock of souvenirs and postcards.

There is a café at Hythe, New Romney and Dungeness, with a limited selection of refreshments (including ice cream) available at Dymchurch station.

The 'last trains board' at Dymchurch station on 14 April 2017.

Jonathan James

Signalling

The railway is controlled from two signal boxes at Hythe and New Romney, with double-line block working in place between Hythe and New Romney.

Between New Romney and Dungeness a 'tablet and ticket' system is in operation, with a red tablet being used for the section between New Romney and Romney Sands and a Green tablet between Romney Sands and Dungeness.

The railway also has an open channel radio system, which is used to communicate between staff on the railway.

Above right: Hythe Signal box seen on 14 April 2017.

Jonathan James

Right: New Romney signal box on 7 May 2018.

Jonathan James

Below: A signaller preparing to hand over a token to No.7 TYPHOON at New Romney on 10 May 2008.

Jonathan James

Level Crossings

The railway has thirteen road crossings as follows. All have now been upgraded with barriers.

Level Crossing	Location
Botolph's Bridge	Between Hythe and Burmarsh Road
Burmarsh Road	Burmarsh Road
Eastbridge Road	Dymchurch
St Mary's Road	Between Dymchurch and St Mary's Bay
Jefferstone Lane	Between St Mary's Bay and Romney Warren
Baldwin Road	Between New Romney and Romney Sands
Seaview Road	Between New Romney and Romney Sands
Romney Sands Road	Romney Sands
Hull Road	Between Romney Sands and Dungeness
Taylor Road	Between Romney Sands and Dungeness
Williamson Road	Between Romney Sands and Dungeness
Battery Road	Between Romney Sands and Dungeness
Dungeness Road	Between Romney Sands and Dungeness

No.12 J.B. SNELL crossing Seaview Road level crossing on 20 August 2015.

Jonathan James

The Permanent Way department have a year-round challenge with maintaining the track and infrastructure, with major track renewals usually undertaken in the winter months. The maintenance team have a number of vehicles including coach 100P, seen above at New Romney on 14 April 2017, and Motor Rail built shunting tractor PW1, pictured below at New Romney on 17 August 2015.

Both: Jonathan James

Rolling Stock Maintenance

The impressive fleet of steam locomotives are fast approaching one-hundred years old and need to be maintained to the highest standard, including a complete overhaul every ten years or so. Several hours before the start of service the steam locomotives need to be prepared, and there is a similar period after the end of service to dampen down the fire and prepare the locomotives for the following day.

No.1 GREEN GODDESS being attended to by her driver at New Romney on 17 August 2015.

Jonathan James

No.3 SOUTHERN MAID being prepared for service on 7 October 2018.

Jonathan James

No.4 THE BUG in the sheds on 7 October 2018.

Jonathan James

No.9 WINSTON CHURCHILL resting inside the sheds at New Romney on 7 October 2018.

Jonathan James

No.8 HURRICANE in the back of the shed on 7 October 2018.

Jonathan James

There is a museum and model railway at New Romney station. The latter is seen on 21 August 2015.

Jonathan James

Coronavirus Specials

Train services were suspended for a long period during 2020 due to the Coronavirus pandemic. The railway was able to reopen on Saturday 4 July 2020, when an hourly service operated between New Romney and Dungeness between 10:30 and 15:30, not calling at Romney Sands. From 18 July services resumed over the whole length of the line, but with pre-booking still a requirement. The railway developed some innovative ticket options to overcome the requirement for pre-booking, including 'Seaside Journeys' between Dungeness and Romney Sands, New Romney and Dungeness or Hythe and Dymchurch in pre-allocated compartments on specified trains. A number of special events also took place, including the annual Bus Rally on 6 September 2020.

The driver of No.5 HERCULES takes a well earned rest between trains whilst standing on the turntable at New Romney on 6 September 2020.

Jonathan James

58

No.6 SAMSON arriving at New Romney with a 'Seaside Journey' on 6 September 2020.

Jonathan James

No.6 SAMSON and No.12 J.B. SNELL at New Romney on 6 September 2020.

Jonathan James

A couple of East Kent buses on display in the car park at New Romney during the annual 'socially distanced' Bus Rally on 6 September 2020 .

Jonathan James

A patriotic No.12 J.B.SNELL, waiting at New Romney between trains on 6 September 2020 .

Jonathan James

No.5 HERCULES being turned at Hythe after working a 'Seaside Journey' from New Romney on 6 September 2020.

Jonathan James

No.5 HERCULES running off the turntable at New Romney, with the Bus Rally in full swing behind on 6 September 2020.

Jonathan James

ROMNEY HYTHE & DYMCHURCH
LIGHT RAILWAY

EXHIBITION OF LOCOMOTIVE
"SOUTHERN MAID"
at WATERLOO STATION, LONDON
(By kind permission of the Southern Railway)

JANUARY 4th-18th, 1947

| 1926 | TO CELEBRATE | 1947 |

The Coming of Age of

The Smallest Public Railway in the World

ROMNEY, HYTHE & DYMCHURCH railway

Chemin de Fer Toursitique
Kleinbahn
Stoomspoorweg

Steam Along With The

BUG CLUB

A Special Club for Children aged 11 and under

ROMNEY, HYTHE & DYMCHURCH RAILWAY

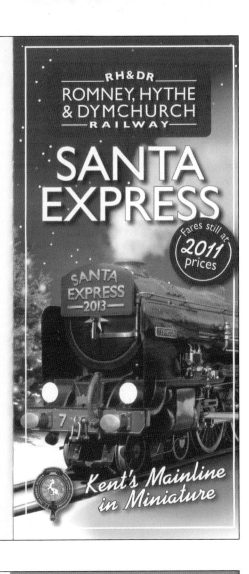

RH&DR
ROMNEY, HYTHE & DYMCHURCH RAILWAY

SANTA EXPRESS

Fares still at 2011 prices

SANTA EXPRESS 2013

Kent's Mainline in Miniature

ROMNEY, HYTHE & DYMCHURCH RAILWAY

TIMETABLE & GUIDE 2001

http://www.rhdr.demon.co.uk

RH&DR
ROMNEY, HYTHE & DYMCHURCH RAILWAY

2006 Timetable and Guide

http://www.rhdr.org.uk

RH&DR
ROMNEY, HYTHE & DYMCHURCH RAILWAY

2007 Timetable and Guide

http://www.rhdr.org.uk

Further Reading

Title	Author	Publisher
Locomotives of the RH&DR	A.R.Crowhurst	Workshop Press, 2004
The Line That Jack Built – A Pictorial Review of the World's Smallest Public Railway	G Freeman Allen	Ian Allan
The Line That Jack Built		Ian Allan
Historical Guide to the Romney, Hythe & Dymchurch Light Railway	C.S.Wolfe	RHDR Association, 1976
Railway World Special – The Romney, Hythe & Dymchurch Railway	J.B.Snell	Ian Allan, 1985
Romney Engines, Carriages & Wagons	Lawson Little	Narrow Gauge Railway Society, 2017
The Romney, Hythe & Dymchurch Railway	R.W.Kidner	Oakwood Press, 1978
R.H.&D.R. – The Kent Coast Line	C.R.J. Hawkins	RHDR
A Miniature Guide to the Romney, Hythe & Dymchurch Railway		RHDR Association, 1981
The World's Smallest Public Railway – A Picture Postcard Journey	Bluecoaster	Plateway Press, 1987
The Romney, Hythe & Dymchurch Railway	W.J.K.Davies	David & Charles, 1988
The Romney, Hythe & Dymchurch Railway	Derek and Barbara Smith	RHDR, 1990
The Romney, Hythe & Dymchurch Railway in Colour	Derek Smith	Ian Allan, 1993
One Man's Railway	J.B.Snell	David St John, 1993
The Romney, Hythe & Dymchurch Railway	Derek Smith	RHDR, 1995
Romneyrail	Vic Mitchell and Keith Smith	Middleton Press, 1999
The Romney, Hythe & Dymchurch Railway – a Visitors Guide	Derek Smith	RHDR, 2001
Romney Remembered – The first 75 years of the Romney, Hythe & Dymchurch Railway		RHDR Association, 2002
The Romney, Hythe & Dymchurch Railway – official Guidebook	Simon Haynes & Tim Godden	RHDR, 2013
Romney Then and Now		RHDR, 2017
A Guide to Dungeness		RHDR